Dear Ray,

Hope you enjoy this).
We both love and admire you
very much.

Love,
Janet & Cheryl
20 09

The Kennedy Brothers

A LEGACY IN PHOTOGRAPHS

The Kennedy Brothers

A LEGACY IN PHOTOGRAPHS

BY **WALTER R. MEARS** AND **HAL BUELL**

Published by Tess Press, an imprint of
Black Dog & Leventhal Publishers, Inc.
151 West 19th Street
New York, NY 10011

Manufactured in the United States

Cover and Interior Design by Red Herring Design

ISBN-13: 978-1-60376-157-4

h g f e d c b

Table of Contents

INTRODUCTION

Four Brothers

They were born to privilege and pressure. At Joseph P. Kennedy's table, the lesson to his four sons put a spin on the cliché of the time, that any American boy could grow up to be president. "Could" was not enough. One of them must grow up to become the first Roman Catholic president of the United States.

One of them did, and was assassinated on the job. Another died trying. A third ran, futilely, after his own personal excesses had undone his best opportunities.

Actually, the father's first choice for a President Kennedy was not his sons—it was himself. He'd made a fortune in finance, in liquor (some said bootlegging during Prohibition), and in Hollywood. When President Franklin D. Roosevelt chose him chairman of the new Securities and Exchange Commission in 1932, critics complained

that he'd put a financial speculator in charge of regulating speculation. FDR is said to have quipped that it took one to know one. Kennedy's three years in that job proved the sardonic point.

In 1937, FDR named Kennedy ambassador to Great Britain, a striking selection because it sent a Boston Irishman to represent America at the starchy, Protestant Court of St. James. Democratic icon Al Smith called Kennedy "Mr. Irish American." It was the role and the stage Kennedy had wanted, but his performance effectively barred his future political way. As Nazi Germany stormed across Eastern Europe at the eve of World War II, Kennedy favored appeasement. He advocated U.S. accommodation with Germany. As the Germans bombed London, he forecast defeat for England.

Still, he came home in 1940 thinking he might become the Democratic presidential nominee, an outside chance at best since he ranked fifth in a poll of potential candidates should FDR not run for a third term. Roosevelt did, foreclosing them all.

The father would not be president. So it must be a son. Joseph P. Kennedy Jr., John F. Kennedy, Robert F. Kennedy, and Edward M. Kennedy were the four sons with five sisters. Their father once called his nine children his hostages to fortune.

It was a cruel fortune: His son and namesake killed in World War II action; JFK assassinated in Dallas; Bobby shot as he celebrated a primary election victory that might have made him the Democratic presidential nominee; Ted the survivor, beset by politically debilitating troubles of his own making, overcame them to become the premier liberal senator of his times, serving up until his death at seventy-seven.

One daughter, Rosemary, mentally disabled and institutionalized until she died. Kathleen killed with her fiancé Peter Wentworth-Fitzwilliam in an airplane crash in France in 1948. Leaving sisters Eunice, Patricia, and Jean to mourn as they had for one brother and would for two more.

Hostages indeed. This is their story. Four stories.

Patrick J. Kennedy, Boston businessman, father of Joseph Kennedy, and grandfather to the four brothers of Joe Kennedy's family. APImages

Ambassador Joe Kennedy with British Prime Minister Winston Churchill after calling on him at Ten Downing Street in London. APImages

Horse-drawn carriages and diplomatic pomp surround Joseph Kennedy, the new American ambassador to England, as he leaves the U.S. Embassy to present his credential to King George VI in March 1938. APImages

ABOVE U.S. Ambassador Kennedy poses with part of his family at Plymouth where they arrived to join him at his ambassadorial post in England. From right: Kathleen; Kennedy; Rose, his wife; Patricia; Jean; Bobby; and Edward in front. Kennedy joked that this was only the first section of his family; he said he didn't want to cause a strain on the English housing situation. Four more Kennedy children would arrive later. APImages

RIGHT John F. (Honey Fitz) Fitzgerald, Boston mayor and father of Rose Fitzgerald, rides in a 1913 parade in Boston. Rose married Joseph Kennedy, uniting political savvy with wealth, and became the mother of the four Kennedy brothers and their five sisters. Honey Fitz was instrumental in the early career of John F. Kennedy.

APImages

ABOVE Proud father Kennedy links arms with his eldest sons, John, left, and Joseph Jr. The young Kennedys arrived at Waterloo station to join the family in London for their summer vacation. APImages

CHAPTER ONE

Joe Jr.

Joseph P. Kennedy Jr. was the first and favorite-son candidate in his politically attuned family. When he was born in 1915, his politician-grandfather said he was a future president. Young Kennedy grew into the ambition. His aim was so obvious that his classmates needled him about it at Harvard and the London School of Economics.

Family connections eased the political way. Grandfather John J. "Honey Fitz" Fitzgerald, the fabled former mayor of Boston, helped him become a delegate to the 1940 Democratic National Convention. Joseph Kennedy Sr. tried to line up support for him to become governor of Massachusetts in 1942.

The script was written, it seemed. But it was written in sand that would not withstand the tide of World War II.

Young Joe was the leader of what he was the first to call "the Kennedy clan," not only because he was the eldest son, but also because he was strong, handsome, and unafraid. In an intensely competitive family—its aggressive touch football would one day become national lore—Joe Jr. was competitor-in-chief. He was an activist rather than an intellectual, determined to excel. He graduated from Harvard with honors and then went on to law school there.

When Joe made up his mind, it stuck. He'd pledged his delegate vote to old-line Democratic manager Jim Farley at the 1940 convention, and he cast it that way despite his father's shaky alliance with President Franklin D. Roosevelt, who wanted a third term. Roosevelt's convention managers called the elder Kennedy in London and asked him to bring his son around. Joe senior said he wouldn't tell junior what to do.

That episode drew public attention to Joe Jr., as did his emergence as a Democratic proponent of isolationism and his opposition to U.S. aid to or intervention against Nazi Germany.

When the activist collided with the theorist, the activist won. FDR declared a state of national emergency in the spring of 1941 to rally U.S. forces against the growing menace of Germany and the Axis allies. Seven months before Pearl Harbor, the threat of war was evident. Joe Jr. had opposed intervention, but he left law school before his final year to volunteer for officer and flight training in the navy. In a letter to his father, there was a hint that his political aspirations were a factor when he wrote that "people will wonder what the devil I am doing back at school when everyone else is working for national defense."

They wouldn't wonder about Joe Kennedy after the shooting started. He flew into the worst of it.

Kennedy earned his pilot's wings in May of 1942. For more than a year his flight duty was routine patrols off Puerto Rico, far from the war zone.

Jack Kennedy was in the Pacific, already the hero of PT 109, before Joe Jr. saw his first combat. Now the senior son would have to prove himself in action. He told a family friend that he'd show them, and in September 1943 he was sent to England to fly Liberator patrol bombers. His squadron flew missions over the Bay of Biscay, off Spain and France, skimming the waves on eight-hour submarine patrols. By May 1944, Joe had flown twenty-five combat missions and was eligible to return home. He declined. He flew in D-Day operations and again was offered home leave. His crew took it.

"He remained," Jack Kennedy wrote, "for he had heard of a new and special assignment for which volunteers had been requested which would require another month of the most dangerous type of flying." It was pushing his luck, but JFK said his brother was preeminently qualified, the odds of returning safely were 50-50, "and Joe never asked for any better odds than that."

The secret mission, in Operation Aphrodite, was his last. That was the code name for a series of bombing runs piloted by skeleton crews who would fly an airplane into position to crash-dive on German rocket-launching sites in France and then parachute to safety. Army missions had failed. Kennedy's was the first navy mission in the operation.

A Liberator dubbed Zootsuit Black was loaded with more than ten tons of explosives. On August 12, 1944, Kennedy and his copilot took off. They were to stay with the bomber until U.S. navigation planes took over radio control to guide the aircraft and crash it into a V-2 German rocket-launching site in Normandy. They were to bail out over England. Two minutes and ten seconds before they were to have parachuted, the flying bomb exploded in the air. What was left of if came down near the village of Blythburgh in Suffolk.

12

An early family portrait of young Joe and John Kennedy, posed with their mother and sisters in 1923. This picture, taken from the Kennedy family album, shows, from left, mother Rose, Eunice, Kathleen, Rosemary, John, and Joe. Kennedy Family Album/APImages.

Of the four brothers, Joe was the most accomplished athlete, winning a place on the Harvard football team and generating interest from professional teams. This 1939 pose shows him on the Harvard freshman team.
APImages

Kennedy was posthumously awarded the Navy Cross, the Distinguished Flying Cross, and the Air Medal. The navy launched the *U.S.S. Joseph P. Kennedy Jr.* in 1946. Brother Robert, by then in the navy, too, was aboard when it first took to sea. The *Kennedy* was one of the ships that enforced the blockade of Cuba during the 1963 missile crisis, the operation ordered by President John F. Kennedy.

In a family memoir after Joe's death, Jack Kennedy wrote, "His worldly success was so assured and inevitable that his death seems to have cut into the natural order of things."

Now that family order would pass to Jack, the second of the brothers.

The competitive spirit, combined with physical fitness, was central to the Kennedy family. In later life their rigorous touch football games at the family home in Hyannis Port, MA, and other places were well known. Here young Joe and John pose with their high school football team in 1927. John sits on the ground at the far right; Joe is in the second row, third from the left.

John F. Kennedy Family Library/APImages

15

By the late 1930s Joseph Kennedy Jr. was being groomed for a career in politics and his father made no secret that he planned for his son to become the first Catholic president of the United States. Here Joe takes time out from a tour of battle fields of the Spanish Civil War to meet with U.S. Embassy staff in Madrid and with a Spanish journalist in 1939. APImages

Joe on a skating date during a vacation in St. Moritz, Switzerland, in January 1939. The woman is skating champion of the period, Megan Taylor. APImages

OPPOSITE

In 1939, as Kennedy sons Joe and John visited European capitals, the talk throughout the continent was about war. John Kennedy, newly returned to the U.S. from London and Berlin, reads the inevitable in a New York newspaper. Outright war moved closer to reality. APImages

By 1941, war engulfed Europe and 25-year-old Joseph Kennedy, center, entered flight school in the U.S. Navy. In this photo he walks with other pilot candidates and an instructor, pointing, at a naval air station near Boston.

APImages

Lt. Joseph Kennedy Jr. escorts his sister Kathleen to the London register office where she would marry Lord Hartington, aka William John Cavendish, in May of 1944. Both Kennedy and Cavendish would die in air crashes, as would Kathleen several years later. APImages

John Kennedy in 1941 while a student at Stanford University's Graduate School of Business after graduating from Harvard. He would soon join the navy, as would his brother Joe, and, later in the war, younger brother Robert.
APImages

Lt. Joseph Kennedy, right, poses with his sister Kathleen, and her husband, William John Cavendish, at their marriage in London in 1944. APImages

OPPOSITE **Lt. John Kennedy,**
on leave in New York in early
1944 after his episode on
PT-109 in the Pacific war.
APImages

Mrs. Rose Kennedy receives the Navy Cross awarded
posthumously to son Joseph who died in action in an air
explosion a year earlier. With Rose at the ceremony is some
of her family, from left: Joseph Kennedy Sr, father of Joe;
Rose Kennedy; Patricia; Edward (Teddy); Admiral Feliz Gygax,
making the award; Robert in background; and Jean.
Robert, by this time, was in navy training. APImages

After World War II, young John F. Kennedy took up the political challenge meant for his brother, Joe. As a candidate for the House of Representatives, John marches behind a banner in a Boston veteran's parade. The banner honored his brother who was killed in a war time explosion. APImages

25

John Kennedy, left, with brother Robert, and dog Mo, at the family home in Hyannis Port, MA, in 1946. John, now 29, had recently won the Democratic nomination for a seat in the House of Representatives from the 11th Massachusetts Congressional district. The Kennedy political saga had begun. APImages

CHAPTER TWO

Jack

So the torch was passed, in the phrase that would one day grace President Kennedy's inaugural address. Jack was heir to the family political mantle.

Joe Jr. had been a natural—hearty, strong, athletic, always one up on Jack when they were boys. JFK had health problems then that continued all his life. He had back trouble. He suffered undiagnosed episodes of pain and unexplained dizzy spells. Eventually, the disease was diagnosed as a chronic adrenal insufficiency and controlled with drugs.

He was the skinny brother, always on medications. Bobby once said that if a mosquito bit Jack, the mosquito would die. JFK would become the active leading man of Washington's Camelot only by overriding his own ailments.

At Harvard, he tried out for the football team but never got past junior varsity before injury and illness sidelined him. (He stuck with college sports, though, and probably was the most talented of presidential golfers when his back let him play.)

As World War II approached, he failed the physicals when he tried to join the army and navy. JFK finally got into the navy with the help of an admiral friend of his father's.

Jack volunteered for duty in the Pacific, and took command of PT-109. On patrol off the Solomon Islands early on August 2, 1943, his craft was rammed apart by a Japanese destroyer. Two crewmen were killed. The survivors made it to a tiny island, one wounded man towed to safety by Jack. They were rescued after Jack carved a message on a coconut shell and gave it to a canoeing islander.

JFK was a hero. PT-109 would become legendary. The episode was the end of his war. He came home on medical leave, suffering from back injuries and from malaria.

Recovered, he began the political career his brother Joe had bequeathed. Jack was elected to Congress in 1946, and easily won two more terms. He then challenged Senator Henry Cabot Lodge Jr., heir to another fabled political name. JFK upset the Republican senator with 51 percent of the vote.

Jack Kennedy married Jacqueline Bouvier in 1953. His worsening back put him on crutches in 1954, and he insisted on surgery despite the risk. It almost killed him and led

John Kennedy at six months, in Brookline, MA, 1917.
John Kennedy National Historic Site

to months of convalescence. During those months, he wrote *Profiles in Courage*, which would win the Pulitzer Prize.

After an attempt at the vice presidential nomination in 1956, Jack was ready to run for president. By the time he announced his candidacy on January 2, 1960, brother Robert and JFK's "Irish Mafia" team of advisers had been at work lining up support.

Jack confronted the issue of his religion as he campaigned. In a September address to the Greater Houston Ministerial Association he stated: "I believe in an America where the separation of church and state is absolute . . . This is the kind of America I believe in and this is the kind I fought for in the South Pacific, and the kind my brother died for in Europe."

With brother Bobby as his campaign manager, Jack defeated Republican Richard M. Nixon in the closest popular vote contest ever. Robert became his attorney general and closest adviser, the only one JFK could trust absolutely. He'd need that support. JFK's thousand days in the White House were marked by international crisis—the failed Bay of Pigs invasion of Cuba, the Soviet

John Kennedy aboard PT-109 in the South Pacific during World War II. John F. Kennedy Library

A young John Kennedy aboard ship as he arrives in New York in September 1938, after a summer vacation in Europe. He was in his junior year at Harvard. APImages

Young John Kennedy, recently returned from World War II in 1946, with Boston Red Sox baseball greats of the period. From left: Ted Williams, Eddie Pellagrini, and Detroit's Hank Greenberg. Pictures like these put John's face on the pages of local newspapers. John F. Kennedy Library

Mayor John F. "Honey Fitz," Fitzgerald, right, the former, affable mayor of Boston at the turn of the century, was instrumental in the early political life of John Kennedy and the youngest of the Kennedy brothers, Edward. The marriage of Rose Fitzgerald, printed dress, and Joseph Kennedy Sr. united two of Boston's politically savvy and wealthy Irish families. From left: Josephine Fitzgerald, John, Rose Fitzgerald Kennedy, and "Honey Fitz." APImages

menace to Berlin, and, most dangerously, the Cuban missile crisis that brought the United States and the Soviet Union to the edge of nuclear war.

The night the missile crisis was settled, Jack said sardonically, "This is the night to go to the theatre, like Abraham Lincoln." Bobby replied that he'd go, too. It was not the only time JFK mused, or joked grimly, about death.

Jack's unfinished presidency was a time of hope, the New Frontier of optimism. Jackie Kennedy's White House gleamed with new décor and glittering social events. JFK promised America would go to the moon within a decade, founded the Peace Corps, signed a nuclear test ban treaty, and spoke eloquently of his aims.

". . . My fellow Americans, ask not what your country can do for you—ask what you can do for your country," he said as he took office. "We need men who can dream of things that never were," he said in Dublin. And in

On the campaign trail, John Kennedy poses with supporters in Cambridge, MA, as he reaches out for the political prize: U.S. House of Representative from the 11th district of Massachusetts. He won. APImages

A victory celebration in 1946 brings John Kennedy together with his campaign workers, and with father, Joseph Kennedy Sr., and mother, Rose. It was Kennedy's first political victory.

APImages

1963, at the Brandenburg Gate in divided Berlin: "Today, in the world of freedom, the proudest boast is 'Ich bin ein Berliner.' "

The words were not always so generous. "Forgive your enemies—but never forget their names," he said, a lesson the Kennedys learned at their father's knee.

"We in this country, in this generation, are—by destiny rather than choice—the watchmen on the walls of world freedom," he said in a speech written but never spoken. Jack was on his way to deliver it in Dallas on November 22, 1963, when he was assassinated by a hidden rifleman, judged to be Lee Harvey Oswald. Kennedy was forty-six. No other president has died so young.

His body lay in repose in the East Room of the White House, the casket closed on Jackie Kennedy's instructions. After a horse-drawn procession to the Capitol, thousands upon thousands waited in lines that stretched through day and night to pay respects to the fallen president.

Then back to the White House for a final family observance before the funeral procession, a parade of the world's royalty and political leaders, from Charles de Gaulle of France to Haile Selassie of Ethiopia. The widow and the brothers, Robert and Edward, walked at the head of the procession.

After Robert Kennedy buried his brother, his grief was so consuming that his friends feared for his health. He did not speak of the assassination by that word, only as a date.

Fittingly, Bobby's most memorable eulogy of Jack was in a political setting, at the Democratic National Convention of 1964. "I realize that as individuals, we can't just look back, that we must look forward," he said, and looked back: "When I think of President Kennedy, I think of what Shakespeare said in *Romeo and Juliet*. 'When he shall die take him and cut him out into stars and he shall make the face of heaven so fine that all the world will be in love with night and pay no worship to the garish sun.'"

34

Jacqueline Bouvier waits while John Kennedy prepares a sailfish for a short ride at Hyannis Port, MA, in June 1953. The couple would marry, making John first of the Kennedy brothers to take a bride. APImages

John F. Kennedy and Jacqueline Bouvier outside the church in Newport, RI, where they were married in September 1953. Kennedy by this time was a Senator from Massachusetts.

APImages

Wedding party hijinks at John Kennedy's wedding reception. Brothers Robert and Edward join in the fun.

Library of Congress

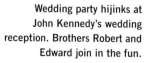

36

The campaign cranks up. John Kennedy addresses
a mass audience at Boston Garden in 1960.

Ed Kelley/Boston Globe/Landov

LEFT John Kennedy makes his way through the hoopla as he arrives for the Democratic National Convention in Los Angeles, in July 1960. He would face Lyndon Johnson for the party's nomination of a presidential candidate. APImages

Robert Kennedy confers with his brother on campaign strategies in July just prior to the Democratic National Convention. Robert managed his brother's campaign, acting as strategist and disciplinarian of the campaign effort. APImages

Standards of the states frame John Kennedy as he stands on the rostrum in the Los Angeles sports arena in July 1960, to address the convention delegates. APImages

Ted Kennedy, key member of the John Kennedy campaign, talks with Speaker Sam Rayburn, who managed Lyndon Johnson's campaign. They met on the floor of the convention in Los Angeles. APImages

A conference underway between Ted Kennedy and the leadership of the Hawaiian delegations to the Democratic Convention. Ted and brother Robert worked the convention floor to convince delegates of John's ability to win the election. APImages

Robert Kennedy shares a whispered conversation with Lyndon Johnson in Johnson's open car as he arrives at the convention site in Los Angeles. APImages

Lyndon Johnson agreed to accept the No. 2 spot on the Democratic ticket and Kennedy stood before the convention delegates on July 15 to formally accept their nomination of him as the Democratic candidate for president. APImages

Kennedy and Johnson, standing side by side, applaud a convention speaker who has just predicted a Democratic victory in the coming presidential election. APImages

**John Kennedy campaigns
in Elgin, IL, in October 1960.**
APImages

Television debates, featuring the candidates face to face in front of a national audience, were held for the first time during the Kennedy/Nixon election in October, 1960. Back and forth the comments went under the hot lights of the TV studio. Kennedy's famed charm and sophisticated wit overshadowed Nixon's more introverted style. Many said that Nixon lost the election on television. APImages

During the television debate Nixon sweated profusely, wiping his face several times, and presenting an image of a man under severe pressure. The TV debate score went to Kennedy, as did the election.
APImages

ABOVE Once Kennedy was elected, he posed in the family's Hyannis Port, MA, home. In this rare photo, all the members of the family were present. Standing from left: Ethel Kennedy; Steve Smith and wife, Jean Kennedy; Senator Kennedy; brother Robert; sister Patricia Lawford; Sargent Shriver; brother Ted's wife, Joan; actor Peter Lawford. In foreground, seated from left are: sister Eunice Shriver; mother Rose; father Joseph; Jacqueline Kennedy; and brother Ted. APImages

John F. Kennedy takes the oath of office administered by Chief Justice Earl Warren and becomes the President of the United States in January 1961. Outgoing President Dwight Eisenhower is at far left; Lyndon Johnson is behind Kennedy; defeated Republican candidate, Richard Nixon, is at right. APImages

ABOVE Kennedy father and son exchange glances at one of the inaugural balls attended by the presidential party the night of January 20, 1961. The election victory and inauguration was the goal that Joe Kennedy Sr. set for his family in the 1930s—that one of his sons become the first Roman Catholic President of the United States. APImages

LEFT A private, tender moment is captured moments after Kennedy completed his inaugural speech and left the podium. His wife, Jackie, tenderly pats his cheek with a word of congratulations. Henry Burroughs/APImages

President Kennedy speaks to a huge crowd in Berlin, June 1963.

Robert Knudsen/John Kennedy Library

BELOW President Charles de Gaulle and John Kennedy stand at the steps of the Élysée Palace during a Kennedy visit to France in October 1961. APImages

RIGHT John Kennedy escorts Russian Premier Nikita Khrushchev to the U.S. embassy in Vienna where they met for the first time in June 1961. APImages

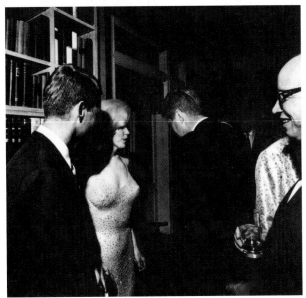

LEFT One of the most talked about incidents of the Kennedy administration was the sultry birthday greeting that actress Marilyn Monroe sang to him at a rally in Madison Square Garden in 1962. The Kennedy brothers, Robert and John, are shown here with Marilyn Monroe at a private party in the Garden after her performance. That's Arthur Schlesinger at right. Landov

ABOVE During his presidency, John Kennedy frequently sought counsel with brother Robert, whom he had named attorney general. Here, in October 1962, they discuss the growing military tension between the U.S. and the Soviet Union that eventually became the Cuban missile crisis. APImages

President Kennedy and his daughter, Caroline, under sail off Hyannis Port, MA, in 1962. John F. Kennedy Library

A Kennedy Family portrait made at Hyannis Port, 1962.
Cecil Stoughton/John Kennedy Library

President Kennedy spends time in a beached boat with his son on a Newport, RI, beach in September 1963.
Landov

John Kennedy kisses his father's forehead during a visit to the family estate at Hyannis Port, MA. The elder Kennedy has suffered a serious disabling stroke by this time. Cecil Stoughton/John Kennedy Library

Jacqueline and John watch the first of the 1962 America's Cup races near Newport, RI, in September. They are aboard the *USS Joseph Kennedy Jr.*, a navy vessel named after Kennedy's older brother killed in World War II.

PREVIOUS PAGE **Caroline and John dance in the Oval Office in time to the clapping hands of the president. The Kennedys, for the first time in decades, brought young children into residence at the White House.** White House Photo

LEFT **John Kennedy plays with his mother's necklace in the White House in August 1962.**

Cecil Stoughton/White House/Landov

Caroline throws up her hands in joy at her first look at a Christmas tree in the White House, trimmed for an employee party.

Henry Burroughs/APImages

Father and son together at the White House in October 1963, just weeks before the president was assassinated in Dallas.

Cecil Stoughton/John Kennedy Library

RIGHT Daddy, aka The President, gets a swinging kiss from son, John Jr., as JFK arrives at Otis Air Force Base, MA, en route to a vacation. Bob Schutz/APImages

FAR RIGHT John greets his father upon the president's return to Washington. Landov

Dinner for Nobel Prize winners of the Western Hemisphere was the occasion for this photo. It was parties such as this that led some to characterize the Kennedy years as Camelot. From left, author Pearl Buck, President Kennedy, Jackie Kennedy, and poet Robert Frost.

OPPOSITE **President John Kennedy aboard the yacht, *Honey Fitz*, in 1963.**

Cecil Stoughton/John Kennedy Library

LEFT **Members of the Kennedy family, led by the president in a golf cart, return to the Hyannis Port, MA, home after an afternoon sail in nearby waters in July 1961. The Hyannis estate housed the spirit of the Kennedy clan. It was there they gathered, in celebration or mourning, to renew spirit and energies.**

John Rous/APImages

Jackie and John Kennedy under sail off Hyannis Port, MA, in July 1960, the summer before he was elected president.

APImages

OPPOSITE President John Kennedy and former President Dwight Eisenhower met at Camp David, the presidential retreat near Thurmont, MD, to discuss the failed Bay of Pigs invasion in April 1961. After posing for the usual pictures, the two men walked to a quiet cabin nearby and were photographed under an overcast sky and a backdrop of trees stripped of their foliage. The photographer said, "They looked so lonely." Paul Vathis/APImages

ABOVE The rocking chair, which favored his ailing back, was a Kennedy trademark in the Oval Office. He was invariably photographed in the chair as he welcomed visitors and colleagues. APImages

Among his favorite pastimes was John Kennedy's press conferences. He took delight in the give and take of his jousts with the media, as in this session in April 1963. APImages

The space program was one of John Kennedy's priorities, his goal being to have an American be the first human on the moon. Here he tours Cape Canaveral in February 1962, with astronaut John Glenn, who was the first American to orbit the earth.

APImages

Dr. Wernher von Braun, left, briefs John Kennedy and Lyndon Johnson at the Saturn assembly plant in Huntsville, AL in September 1962.

APImages

**President Kennedy reaches out to the crowd at Fort Worth, TX,
as he arrives for a visit to the state in November 1963.**

Cecil Stoughton/John Kennedy Library

The president's limousine rushes off with Secret Service agent Clint Hill on the bumper seconds after President Kennedy was fatally shot in Dallas in November 1963. Kennedy slumps in the seat, and Jackie bends over him.

APImages/Ike Altgens

Lee Harvey Oswald, who assassinated President John Kennedy.

APImages

By day and by night
mourners lined up to
pay a final visit to John
Kennedy. APImages

John Kennedy's coffin lies in
state in the Capitol,
November 1963. APImages

Jacqueline Kennedy kisses
the flag-draped coffin of her
husband as her daughter,
Caroline, kneels nearby in the
rotunda of the Capitol. APImages

The statue of Abraham
Lincoln stands ghostlike in
the background with hand
outstretched toward the
Kennedy coffin in the Capitol
rotunda. Harry Harris/APImages

Jacqueline Kennedy, escorted by Kennedy
brothers Robert and Edward, arrives for a
funeral Mass at St. Matthew's Cathedral in
Washington, in November 1963. Also in
the group are Sargent Shriver and President
and Mrs. Lyndon Johnson. APImages

A caisson bearing the flag-draped coffin of President Kennedy pauses in front of the Capitol in Washington en route to burial at Arlington National Cemetery. APImages

Little John Kennedy offers a salute as the coffin carrying his father passes by in Washington in November 1963. Also in the picture is President Kennedy's widow, Jacqueline, and the president's brothers, Edward and Robert. Daughter Caroline stands with her mother. APImages

ABOVE Honor Guard prepares
to fold the U.S. flag for the widow
of President Kennedy at the burial site
in Arlington National Cemetery
in November 1963.

Abbie Rowe/Park Service/John Kennedy Library

LEFT Jacqueline Kennedy accepts
the folded flag that covered John
Kennedy's coffin during the burial
ceremony at Arlington National
Cemetery in November 1963.

Eddie Adams/APImages

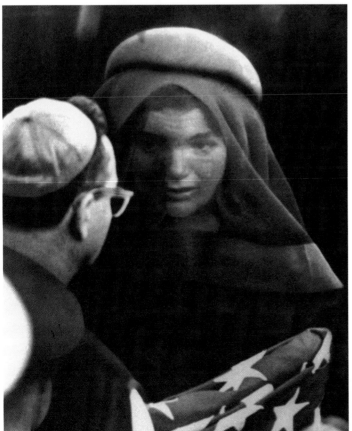

CHAPTER THREE

Bobby

Robert F. Kennedy had been JFK's inside man, and by 1960 he wanted to launch an independent political career of his own. But his brother came first. The family nickname, Bobby, belied his toughness: He was the manager and counselor, enforcing order and discipline in John F. Kennedy's campaigns and as his attorney general.

After Dallas, Bobby was an uncomfortable and unwelcome member of Lyndon B. Johnson's cabinet. Bobby had not wanted LBJ on the ticket in 1960. Jack insisted, saying he was not going to die in office so the vice presidency would be meaningless. In 1963, the choice of LBJ changed the course of American politics and of Robert Kennedy's life.

Like his brothers, he went to Harvard. He earned his law degree at the University of Virginia. In 1950 he married Ethel Skakel, the mother of his eleven children.

Robert Kennedy worked in the Justice Department in 1951, resigned to manage John Kennedy's 1952 Senate campaign, and then, with his father as sponsor, became assistant counsel of Republican Senator Joseph R. McCarthy's Communist-baiting Senate investigations subcommittee. McCarthy and Joe Kennedy were old friends. Robert quit after eight months and later became counsel for the committee's Democratic minority.

In 1957, he became the crusading chief counsel of a Senate committee that investigated labor

73

union racketeering that went after the Teamsters Union and its boss, Jimmy Hoffa. He resigned in 1959 to manage his brother's presidential campaign.

As Jack's attorney general, he tackled Hoffa again, went after organized crime, and led the drive for civil rights, enforcing desegregation against Southern defiance. In 1962, he sent U.S. marshals to protect Freedom Riders in Montgomery, Alabama, and later, to enforce a federal court order admitting a black student to the University of Mississippi. They had to be backed with troops to quell the riots that followed, and two people were killed.

After his brother was assassinated, Robert would stay only briefly in the cabinet of a president he considered a pretender. Lyndon Johnson, in kind, thought him a threat. Johnson went to the awkward length of ruling out all of the members of his cabinet as vice presidential prospects to signal that Robert Kennedy would not be on his ticket.

Two days later, Bobby resigned as attorney general to run for the Senate in New York. It was a difficult campaign. He did not have his brother's ease on the campaign platform, his ties to New York were tenuous, and he was attacked as a carpetbagger. Opponents said he was arrogant and ruthless—a reputation that had grown with his role as political disciplinarian in service to JFK.

Even so, he won the seat, and joined brother Edward M. Kennedy, already a senator.

Years before, recuperating from back surgery, Jack Kennedy had said, "Just as I went into politics when Joe died, if anything happened to me tomorrow my brother Bobby would run for my seat. And if anything happened to him, my brother Teddy would run for us."

So it was, practically if not precisely.

Civil rights legislation, minority neighborhood needs, and the plight of the poorest Americans were his specialties in the Senate. He visited South Africa in 1966 where he said, "Each time a man stands up for an ideal, or acts to improve the lot of others, or strikes out against injustice, he sends forth a tiny ripple of hope." Robert became increasingly dismayed at U.S. policy in the Vietnam War. As president, Jack Kennedy had supported U.S. involvement, but Robert Kennedy changed course, opposed the use and escalation of American combat troops, and broke with LBJ on the conflict.

By the autumn of 1967, anti-war Democrats were looking for a credible candidate to challenge Johnson in the coming campaign. They wanted Robert Kennedy, but he wouldn't answer. Senator Eugene J. McCarthy of Minnesota became their candidate. After McCarthy had come close to upsetting the president in the New Hampshire primary and was on the way to defeating him in Wisconsin, Robert declared his own candidacy in mid-March. Again he was assailed as a ruthless opportunist. He said he had ended his earlier indecision because the country was "on a perilous course" and he was obliged to do all that he could. Johnson quit the race at the end of that month.

Robert and McCarthy competed through the spring presidential primaries, with Bobby gaining the advantage until McCarthy upset him in Oregon, the first time a Kennedy had lost any election.

In climactic California, Robert won the primary and a push toward the presidential nomination at the Democratic National Convention. "On to Chicago," he rallied his supporters. He would

Robert Kennedy, with his sister Jean on board, paddles his small boat at an unknown location. The boat's name, *Bobby*, refers to Robert's nickname which stuck with him throughout his life.

Kennedy Family Album/APImages

Vigorous sport was part of the Kennedy clan routine. Posing here in 1941 behind the tennis court net at the family estate in Palm Beach, FL, are, from left: Eunice, Bobby, Teddy, and Jean. APimages

In June 1950, Robert F. Kennedy married Ethel Skakel at St. Mary's Roman Catholic church in Greenwich, CT. The marriage of Robert and Ethel, who was active in her husband's political career, produced 11 children, the largest family of the Kennedy clan. APimages

not get there. A gunman was waiting in the kitchen of the Ambassador Hotel, a shortcut exit after Bobby's victory rally in the ballroom. Sirhan Bishara Sirhan shot him in the head, and he died early on the morning of June 6, 1968.

The unthinkable had happened twice within five years. Three of the four Kennedy brothers were dead; one in war, two murdered. Now it was Ted Kennedy's time to deliver the eulogy. "My brother need not be idealized or enlarged in death beyond what he was in life," he said, ". . . a good and decent man who saw wrong and tried to right it, saw suffering and tried to heal it, saw war and tried to end it."

After the funeral Mass, a train carried Kennedy's body past throngs of people standing in the dark along the tracks and crowding the stations between New York and Washington.

Robert Kennedy was buried by the light of the moon and the eternal flame at the grave of his brother the president.

OPPOSITE Bobby, left, and Ted, on a skiing vacation in Stowe, VT, in December 1960. John Kennedy had won the presidential election and had named Robert as attorney general. The brothers awaited the January inauguration to begin their administration. APimages

77

Robert Kennedy and Supreme Court Justice William O. Douglas turn out in ceremonial robes for a souvenir picture during a visit to Stalingrad in the late summer of 1955. The two were in a party that visited Siberia and other Asian points. APimages

OPPOSITE It's dinner time at the home of Robert Kennedy in McLean, VA, in June 1960, just ahead of the national political conventions and the presidential election. Robert had just been named Father of the Year. Clockwise, from lower left: Kerry, Michael, Joe, Bobby, father Robert, David, Courtney, Kathleen, and mother Ethel. APimages

BELOW Attorney General Robert Kennedy pilots the sailboat *Victura* through Hyannis Port, MA, waters during a vacation sail with his family in July 1961. From left: Maria Shriver, Courtney Kennedy, Bobby Schriver, Robert Kennedy Jr., Pat Prusyewski, Robert, David Kennedy, and Kathleen Kennedy. APimages

Senator Robert Kennedy, center foreground, stands near a memorial black flag he planted on the summit of Mt. Kennedy in the Yukon. The Canadian government named the 13,900 foot mountain after the assassinated American president. Kennedy and a group of experienced climbers scaled the peak in March 1965, the first Americans to reach the summit. Doug Wilson/APImages

OPPOSITE Robert Kennedy pulls on a towline to free a stuck plane at the base camp of Mt. Kennedy prior to climbing the mountain.

Doug Wilson/APImages

The Kennedy brothers in white tie and tails at the annual Gridiron Club dinner in Washington in March 1958. John, center, was a senator at this time; Edward, left, a student at the University of Virginia; and Robert was chief counsel to the Senate Rackets Committee. The dinner is an annual affair to roast politicians and journalists in the capital. APimages

Robert Kennedy and James R. Hoffa, president of the Teamsters union, exchange comments in the hearing room in September 1958, where Hoffa's activities as union boss were under investigation. Man in center is Walter J. Sheridan, a committee investigator. APimages

Robert, Edward, and John Kennedy confer during a committee hearing in Washington in 1959. At this time Robert was counsel for the Senate Rackets Committee. APimages

Ted Kennedy and Robert Kennedy, who managed the election campaign of his brother John, watch election results the night of November 8, 1960, at Robert's house in Hyannis Port, MA. At left is Larry O'Brien, election campaign staffer. At right, Patricia Kennedy Lawford, by this time married to actor Peter Lawford. APimages

Robert Kennedy in a relaxed position in his office at the Department of Justice as he listens to a 2:15 a.m. phone-in first hand report on the race violence situation in Montgomery, AL, May 1961. APimages

ABOVE Robert Kennedy, now the attorney general, addresses protestors outside the Justice Department in Washington. The demonstrators claimed that there was not a sufficient number of minorities being hired in the Justice Department.

Library of Congress

RIGHT Kennedy gets advice from his first assistant Harold Reis in May 1961 on the next course of action to take in the Montgomery, AL, riots over segregation.

APimages

By October 1964, Robert Kennedy had resigned his cabinet post and began his campaign for the U.S. Senate seat from New York. It was a tough fight; Kennedy was seen as a carpetbagger. Here he talks to a street gathering in New York's garment district. He won the election.

Robert Wands/APImages

OPPOSITE **Senator Robert Kennedy holding a news conference at Columbia University, in New York, May 1967.** CBS-TV/Landov

Robert Kennedy visits the grave of his slain brother at Arlington cemetery on January 20, 1965. APimages

Ted and Robert Kennedy confer
during a hearing in Washington
of the Senate labor committee,
March 1967. APimages

OPPOSITE Robert and Ted
Kennedy, both senators
in October 1965, on the steps
of the capitol. APimages

Senator Robert Kennedy talks with a group at a country store in the Mississippi Delta near Greenville in April 1967. With three other senators he visited the area to investigate the federal anti-poverty program. Jack Thornell/APImages

Ted and Robert attend the World Series at Fenway Park in Boston, March 1967.

Joe Dennehy/Boston Globe/Landov

Philosophically, Kennedy broke with Lyndon Johnson after the death of his brother. After several years as a senator, he wondered whether or not to enter the race for the presidency. He tested the sentiment of the black community toward his campaign and described his platform to, among others, this group in the Watts section of Los Angeles in March 1968. APimages

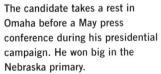

The candidate takes a rest in Omaha before a May press conference during his presidential campaign. He won big in the Nebraska primary.

Larry Stoddard/APImages

Robert Kennedy rides through Detroit during his presidential campaign, attracting a large crowd of black youths in May 1968 during his campaign for president. His wife, Ethel, rides with him in the open car.

Preston Stroup/APImages

Brother Ted joins Robert Kennedy in a Boston parade in March 1968. Paul Connell/Boston Globe/Landov

Bobby Kennedy on his presidential campaign in 1968. Burton Berinsky/Landov

An old-fashioned whistle stop speech is the
feature of Kennedy's presidential campaign as
speaks from the back of the Wabash Canonball
at Peru, IN, in April 1968. APImages

At another whistle stop in Wabash,
IN, Kennedy spoke to a train side
crowd, April 1968. APImages

Kennedy and his dog, Freckles, go for a stroll on the beach near Astoria, OR, during his campaign for the Democratic presidential nomination in May 1968.

A huge crowd at the Ambassador Hotel in Los Angeles cheers Robert Kennedy, with his wife, Ethel, at his side, after the primary victory in California. "On to Chicago," he said. Moments later he was assassinated.

Dick Strobel/APImages

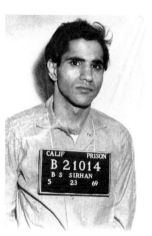

Robert Kennedy lies mortally wounded in the Ambassador Hotel in Los Angeles. Kennedy was shot as he walked through the hotel's kitchen to leave.

Bill Eppridge/LIFE/TimeInc

Sirhan Bishara Sirhan, who assassinated Robert Kennedy.

APImages

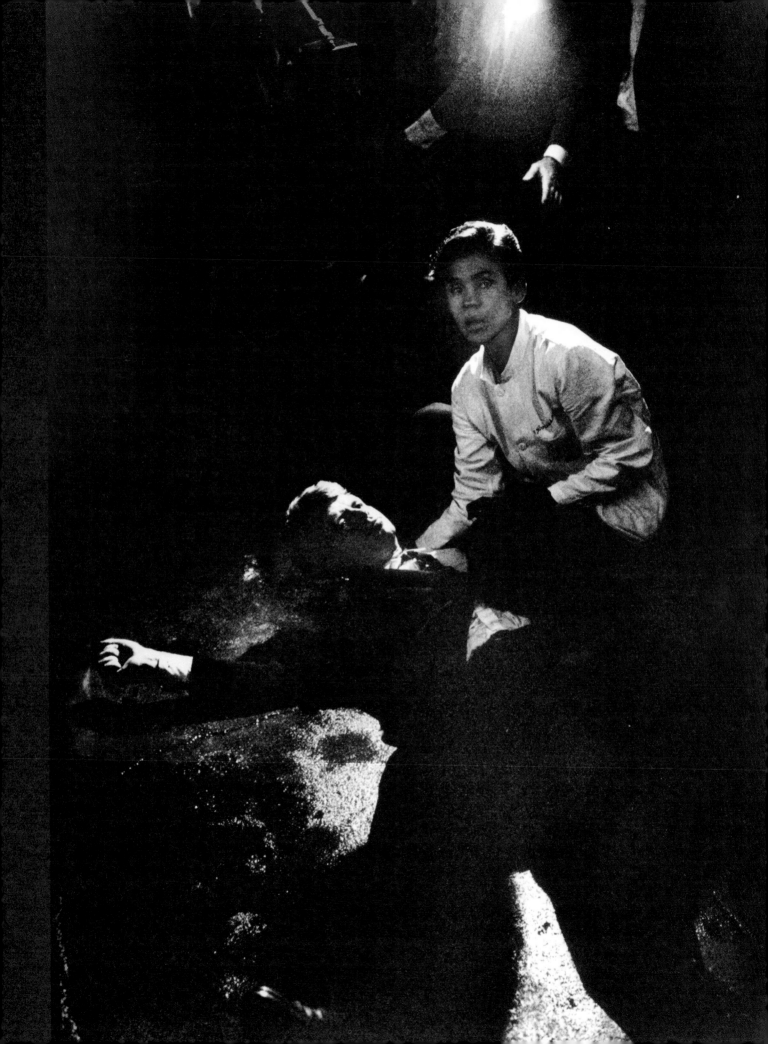

OPPOSITE **Pallbearers carry the casket and body of Robert Kennedy from St. Patrick's Cathedral on June 8, 1968, in New York to begin its travel to Washington and Arlington National Cemetery where Kennedy was buried.** APImages

RIGHT **Ethel Kennedy and Edward Kennedy arrive at their pew in St. Patrick's Cathedral.** APImages

BELOW **Edward Kennedy stands at the altar of St. Patrick's Cathedral in New York to deliver the eulogy for his brother. Lyndon Johnson sits next to the flag draped coffin.** APImages

Pallbearers carry the coffin of Robert Kennedy to its burial place the night of June 8, 1968, at Arlington National Cemetery. APImages

The final brother, Edward Kennedy, sits with his mother, Rose, and his father, Joseph Sr., who had suffered a stroke, at the family's Hyannis Port, MA, home, soon after the June burial of Robert. APImages

CHAPTER FOUR

Ted

Edward M. Kennedy was an unlikely candidate for patriarch, of either the Kennedy family or the United States Senate. That he became both was a testament to fate and to political perseverance.

Ted was the ebullient baby of the family. A mediocre student, he followed the Kennedy tradition to Harvard, where he got himself suspended as a freshman by having a friend take his Spanish test for him. He enlisted in the U.S. Army, served two years in Germany, and re-entered Harvard in 1953.

Ted played football there, as his brothers had, and outdid them. As a starting end, he was impressive enough to draw a pro football inquiry. He declined, saying he was going into "another contact sport—politics."

After law school at the University of Virginia, he did so, in Jack's campaigns for the Senate in 1958 and for president in 1960. He handled the western states and, after JFK was elected, talked of staying there to make his own way instead of being "constantly compared with two brothers of such superior ability."

But family ties and his father's insistence called him back to Massachusetts to succeed the Senate seat JFK resigned to become president. Ted wasn't thirty yet, not old enough to be a senator, so he had to wait. While he did, he served as an assistant district attorney in Boston at a token $1 a year. Jack arranged to get a friend appointed for the two years until Ted could run.

Ted won a partial term in 1962. He would later

ABOVE Edward Kennedy reaches for a volleyball during a match with media types at an informal gathering in September 1981, at the family estate in Hyannis Port, MA. The Kennedys regularly invited press for picnic-type soirees. J. Walter Green/APImages

LEFT Wedding day for Edward Kennedy at St. Joseph's Roman Catholic church in Bronxville, NY, November 1958. The bride is Joan Bennett. The couple would have three children; the marriage would end in divorce. Jack Harris/APImages

be re-elected eight times. After Bobby was elected senator from New York in 1964, he and Ted were sworn in together. Ted was using a gold-headed cane, his back in a brace, still recuperating from the injuries he'd suffered in the crash of a chartered light plane on the way to the Massachusetts Democratic convention seven months earlier.

He reminded Bobby that he'd won Senate election by a far wider margin. But the senior senator was the junior brother, and he told his aides he'd play it that way, in second spot.

Ted was the legislator, deferential to the customs of the Senate. Bobby was the impatient, a quotable figure at public hearings, a U.S. and world traveler, a potential president in waiting.

When he challenged President Johnson in 1968, Ted once again worked in the presidential quest of an elder brother, and was on campaign duty in San Francisco when Bobby was assassinated in Los Angeles. At his memorial, he said, "Those of us who loved him and who take him to his rest today, pray that what he was to us and what he wished for others will someday come to pass for all the world."

Stricken, he took refuge in Hyannis Port and in the solitude of sailing the waters off Cape Cod. He'd always had a hail-fellow affinity for a drink or two; now that became part of his retreat.

Edward Kennedy poses for a football picture in 1955 during his playing days at Harvard.

He said no to party leaders who wanted to draft him for the 1968 ticket. Returning to the Senate, he challenged the deputy Democratic leader and won that job in 1969. But the mundane duties of the party whip didn't fit his style, and he was ousted two years later.

By then he had driven into the worst personal crisis of his life, the accident that killed Mary Jo Kopechne on Chappaquiddick Island off Martha's Vineyard on July 18, 1969. They'd left together after a party with former Robert Kennedy campaign staffers. Ted was driving when the car went off a bridge into the water. She died in the car.

Ted said he'd made repeated attempts to rescue her before swimming to safety and leaving the scene. He did not call police until her body had been discovered the next day. Ted pleaded guilty to leaving the scene of an accident and got a two-month suspended jail sentence.

Until then he'd been a leading prospect for the 1972 presidential nomination. Chappaquiddick ended that and led him to say in a nationally televised address a week later that he had considered resigning from the Senate. He also said that he'd wondered "whether some awful curse did actually hang over all the Kennedys."

Edward Kennedy, like his brothers before him, entered the political world early. Here he campaigns in March 1962, to be the Democratic nominee for the U.S. Senate seat left vacant by his brother, then president. He faced a formidable opponent in Attorney General Edward J. McCormack Jr., nephew of House Speaker John W. McCormack. Kennedy prevailed.

J. Walter Green/APImages

Despite it all, he won landslide re-election in Massachusetts in 1970. But there would be no third Kennedy running for president in 1972 or 1976. When Ted did run, it was against Democratic President Jimmy Carter. He won enough primaries to keep campaigning into the 1980 Democratic National Convention, forcing liberal planks into the party platform before he yielded.

Away from the Senate, his personal habits were erratic. His marriage to Joan Bennett was foundering over his drinking and affairs and her alcoholism. They were divorced late in 1982.

A decade later, after a stern stop-drinking lecture from a Republican colleague and his second marriage to Victoria Reggie, the patriarchal Ted Kennedy emerged. He was second in Senate seniority, a committee chairman who had put his liberal imprint on legislation for decades.

Then, on May 17, 2008, he was felled by a malignant brain tumor. Despite it, he returned to the Senate and to the political stage for one last hurrah, at the Democratic convention in Denver.

"The torch will be passed again, to a new generation of Americans," he said in that vale-dictory. ". . . The work begins anew. The hope rises again. And the dream lives on."

Ted Kennedy died on August 25, 2009, at his home in Hyannis Port, only fourteen days after the death of his sister, Eunice. At seventy–seven he had been a senator longer than any of his three brothers had lived.

OPPOSITE **After defeating McCormack for the Democratic nomination, Edward faced George Cabot Lodge, son of Henry Cabot Lodge, former Ambassador to the United Nations. Kennedy went on to win the Senate seat and Henry Cabot Lodge soon thereafter was named as John Kennedy's Ambassador to South Vietnam in the early years of American involvement in Southeast Asia.** APImages

Kennedy brothers, center, sit together during the State of the Union address by President Lyndon Johnson in January 1965. Edward was senior to Robert, who was in his freshman year. Robert had resigned as Johnson's attorney general after John Kennedy was assassinated, and was later elected as a senator from New York. APImages

Touch football was part of the scene when the Kennedys got together, or when they gathered members of the press at the compound in Hyannis Port, MA. Here, in September 1966, Ted Kennedy scores a touchdown.

Ed Fitzgerald/Boston Globe/Landov

OPPOSITE **His victory in the November 1964 election was celebrated in a hospital where Edward Kennedy was recuperating from a back injury suffered in a plane crash. With him are his wife, Joan, daughter, Kara, and son, Edward Jr.** Bill Chaplis/APImages

The Kennedy Brothers, in August 1963, pose in Washington: Attorney General Robert, Senator Edward, and President John. APImages

Edward Kennedy visits a
Special Forces camp in
Vietnam in October 1965.

Edward Kennedy's car is pulled from a pond at Edgartown, MA, in July 1969. The car, with Kennedy driving and with Mary Jo Kopechne as passenger, plunged off the bridge. The two had left a nearby party for political party workers in the various Kennedy campaigns. Kopechne drowned and Kennedy survived. The incident remained a shadow over Edward's career. APImages

Mary Jo Kopechne
APImages

Edward and his wife, Joan, walk past a line of mourners after the burial of Mary Jo Kopechne in Plymouth, PA, in July 1969. APImages

TED

Ted Kennedy, his wife, Joan, and their children, Kara and Edward Jr., walk the beach in Hyannis Port, MA, in November 1969. The Kennedys gathered in Hyannis Port to attend memorial services for Kennedy patriarch Joe Kennedy Sr., who died November 18 at the age of 81. APImages

OPPOSITE
Edward Kennedy swims with members of a Boston Babe Ruth Baseball team. Kennedy opened his pool in McLean, VA, to the team, which was playing in a championship game nearby. J. Scott Applewhite/ APImages

Senator Edward Kennedy, the last of four brothers, leaves Old St. Stephen's Church in Boston, behind the coffin of his mother, Rose. She died in January 1995 at the age of 104.

Elise Amendola/APImages

Throughout the history of the Kennedy clan, Hyannis Port, MA, was the family homestead, the place for relaxation, where tragedy was healed and energy renewed. Ted Kennedy and family preparing to sail, July 1972. Phil Preston/Boston Globe/Landov

A wind-tossed Edward Kennedy strolls along the Hyannis Port Harbor in September 1985, where he had earlier watched sailing races. Mark Lennihan/APImages

Edward Kennedy Jr. rides atop his father as they slide down a snowy hillside at their home in McLean, VA, on Christmas Eve, 1973. Young Edward's leg was amputated weeks earlier in order to arrest bone cancer. APImages

Edward Kennedy and an aid walk past a huge English elm tree in June 1978, on Capitol Hill before it was cut down because of Dutch elm disease. Kennedy wrote a eulogy to the tree, which was inserted in the Congressional Record citing John Kennedy's reference to it as the Humility Tree. Politicians had to bow their head to duck under its low limbs as they passed by.

ABOVE After Kennedy announced that
he would take on Jimmy Carter for the
1980 Democratic Party nomination for
president he greeted spectators outside
Boston's Faneuil Hall in November 1979.
APImages

LEFT Joan greets Kennedy after he
addressed the Democratic Convention in
Madison Square Garden in August 1980.
APImages

Masschusetts Democratic power duet—Speaker of the House Tip O'Neill and Senator Edward Kennedy—share a laugh before addressing senior citizens at a health care gathering in Washington in October 1979. John Duricka/ APImages

Party time in Boston features Ted Kennedy and his wife, Victoria Reggie, celebrating an election victory after his November 9 win.

Pat Greenhouse/Boston Globe/Landov

OPPOSITE
The candidate at work— Edward Kennedy greets the crowd at the Democratic Convention in New York's Madison Square Garden in August 1980. He looked to beat Jimmy Carter for the party's presidential nomination.

Cameron Bloch/APImages

Some years after his divorce
from wife Joan, Kennedy
married Victoria Reggie
Kennedy. The couple is shown
here during a December
2008 ceremony at Harvard
to present Kennedy with an
honorary degree.

Steven Senne/APImages

Edward and Victoria in front
of houses inside the Kennedy
compound in Hyannis Port
in September 1992.

Susan Walsh/APImages

ABOVE **Hillary Clinton and Edward Kennedy in September 1999. The Clintons and Kennedys were close political allies, but the ground shifted when Kennedy supported Barack Obama in 2009.**

Joe Marquette/APImages

ABOVE **Ted Kennedy confers with members of both parties in March 2006, on immigration reforms under discussion in the Senate. From left: Barack Obama, Diane Feinstein, John McCain, Joe Lieberman, and Kennedy.** Larry Downing/Reuters/Landov

LEFT **Ted Kennedy worked closely with his colleagues over the years in the Senate, as in this confidential exchange with Senator Joseph Biden during Patriot Act hearings in October 2003.**

Gerald Herbert/APImages

Barack Obama shares a laugh with Ted Kennedy during a rally at American University in Washington in January 2008. Obama had plenty to smile about. Kennedy endorsed Obama's candidacy for Democratic Party nomination for president. Chuck Kennedy/MCT/Landov

Kennedy and Victoria, with their dogs Sunny and Splash, arrive on Capitol Hill in Washington in November 2008.

Lauren Victoria Burke/APImages

Politics were always in the wind in Massachusetts as here, the start of a sail from Martha's Vineyard in August 1997, aboard the Kennedy sailboat *Mya*. Sailors include President Bill Clinton, Ted Kennedy, First Lady Hillary Clinton, and Representative Patrick Kennedy.

Gregg Gibson/APImages

136

ABOVE It's thumbs up from Ted Kennedy in May 2008, as he leaves Massachusetts General Hospital, Boston, after a five day stay for examination of a brain tumor. He was accompanied by his family; Caroline Kennedy Schlossberg, daughter of John Kennedy, is at right.

George Rizer/Boston Globe/Landov

RIGHT Ted Kennedy is all smiles as he takes his seat at the inauguration of Barack Obama in Washington, January 2009. Win McNamee/Bloomberg/Landov

NEXT PAGE The crowd roared its approval of Senator Edward Kennedy at the end of his speech to the 2008 Democratic Party Convention in Denver.

Stephen Savoia/APImages

Ted Kennedy and his wife, Victoria, aboard their sailboat *Mya* at Hyannis Port, MA, on a chilly day in May 2008.

Matthew J. Lee/Boston Globe/Landov

Ted and Victoria Kennedy go for a walk with their dogs at the Kennedy home in Hyannis Port, MA, in May 2008. The senator had recently checked out of the hospital where he had been diagnosed with a brain tumor.

Steven Senne/APImages

Ted Kennedy stands near a wall display featuring the famous quote from his brother John, which was delivered in John's inaugural speech decades ago. The quote was inscribed at a school Kennedy visited in January 1996, to meet with students who had received a humanitarian award. Dan Loh/APImages

Index